The Kite That Flew Away

Written by Joanna Austin
Illustrated by Anni Matsick

Adams 12 Five Star Schools
1500 E 128th Avenue
Thornton, CO 80241
(720) 972-4000

Aunt Sue was making a gift for Annie.
She got blue paper and green paper.
She got sticks and string and glue.

3

First she cut the blue paper.
Then she put on some glue.
"What will it be?" said Annie.
"Please give me just one little clue."

"Here's one little clue," said Aunt Sue.
"This is something to use outside."
She drew some lines and dots on the paper.

5

"I still don't know what it is," said Annie.
"Can you give me one more clue?"
"Watch this," said Aunt Sue.
She put together the paper and the sticks
and a long, long string.

"It's a kite!" said Annie.
"A new kite! Let's go fly it!"

7

Annie and Aunt Sue took the kite outside.

The kite flew up in the air.

The wind blew and blew.

The kite flew and flew.

Just then, the string broke.
The kite flew away.
Aunt Sue and Annie ran after it.
But they couldn't catch it.

The wind blew and blew.
The kite flew and flew.
Where was it going?

It flew over the lake.
It flew over a boat.
But no one could catch the kite.

The wind blew and blew.
The kite flew and flew.
Where was it going?

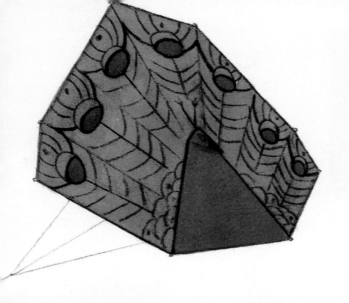

It flew over the woods and back to the town.
Then the wind stopped, and the kite fell.

Down, down, down came Annie's new kite.
It came down right in Aunt Sue's yard.
"It's my kite! My new blue kite!" said Annie.

"Oh, Aunt Sue," she said. "Look."

"Don't worry," said Aunt Sue.
"We just need a little more paper and
a little more glue.
This kite will look as good as new!"